D0484699

PRESENT MOMENT
WONDERFUL MOMENT

PRESENT MOMENT
WONDERFUL MOMENT

Mindfulness Verses for Daily Living

THICH NHAT HANH

Drawings by Mayumi Oda

Parallax Press
Berkeley, California

Parallax Press
P.O. Box 7355
Berkeley, California 94707

Translated from the Vietnamese by Annabel Laity.

Cover drawing by Mayumi Oda. Photo on back cover by David Foecke.
Composed on Macintosh IIcx, in Palatino 11/14, by Parallax Press.
Edited by Therese Fitzgerald, Wendy Johnson, and Arnold Kotler.

Library of Congress Cataloging in Publication Data
Nhat Hanh, Thich.
  [Tùng buóc no hoa sen. English]
  Present moment wonderful moment: mindfulness
verses for daily living / Thich Nhat Hanh; illustrated by
Mayumi Oda.
     p. cm.
  Translation of Tùng buóc no hoa sen
  ISBN 0-938077-21-X
  1. Buddhism— Prayer-books and devotions—English.
I. Title.
BQ5578. V58N4713   1990
294.3'443—dc20
                                                    90-37062
                                                    CIP

Contents

Verses for Starting the Day

Verses for Meditation

Verses for Eating Mindfully

Verses for Other Daily Activities

Introduction

W hen I entered the Tu Hiêu Monastery as a novice in 1942, I received a copy of *Gathas for Everyday Use*, compiled by the Chinese meditation master Du Ti. *Gathas* are short verses which we can recite during our daily activities to help us dwell in mindfulness. Du Ti's book of fifty gathas was written for monks and nuns of former times. At Plum Village, where I live in France, we practice gathas when we wake up, when we enter the meditation hall, during meals, and when we wash the dishes. In fact, we recite gathas silently throughout the entire day to help us attend to the present moment. During the summer of 1982, in order to help the children and adults at Plum Village practice mindfulness, we began assembling gathas relevant for life today. The result is this handbook of practical, down-to-earth verses.

We often become so busy that we forget what we are doing or even who we are. I know someone who says he even forgets to breathe! We forget to look at the people we love and to appreciate them, until it is too late. Even when we have some leisure time, we don't know how to get in touch with what is going on inside and outside of ourselves. So we turn on the television or pick up the telephone as if we might be able to escape from ourselves.

To meditate is to be aware of what is going on—in our bodies, our feelings, our minds, and in the world. When we settle into the present moment, we can see beauties and wonders right before our eyes—a newborn baby, the sun rising in the sky. We can be very happy just by being aware of what is in front of us.

One way to help us dwell in the present moment is to practice reciting gathas or mindfulness verses. When we focus our mind on a gatha, we return to ourselves and become more aware of each action. When the gatha ends, we continue our activity with heightened awareness. When we drive a car, signs can help us find our way. The sign and the road become one, and we see the sign all along the way until the next sign. When we practice with gathas, the gathas and the rest of our life become one, and we live our entire lives in awareness. This helps us very much, and it helps others as well. We find that we have more peace, calm, and joy, which we can share with others.

As exercises in both meditation and poetry, gathas are very much in keeping with the Zen tradition. When you memorize a gatha, it will come to you quite naturally, for example, when you turn on the water or drink a cup of tea. But it is not necessary to learn all the verses at once. You can begin with one or two and learn more over time. After some time you may find that you have learned all of them and are even creating your own. Composing new verses is a way of enriching the tradition. When I wrote the gathas for using the telephone and driving a car, I did so within the tradition which I inherited from my teachers. Many of these gathas are translations from Vietnamese. If you find a word or a sentence you can improve, please send your recommendation to the author, in care of the publisher, and each new edition of this book will be fresher and more relevant. If you compose a new verse, please send it to us together with a commentary, like the ones in this book. I hope you find this collection of gathas a steady and delightful companion.

nhat hanh
April 1990

VERSES FOR STARTING THE DAY

1. WAKING UP

Waking up this morning, I smile.
Twenty-four brand new hours are before me.
I vow to live fully in each moment
and to look at all beings with eyes of compassion.

If you really know how to live, what better way to start the day than with a smile? Your smile affirms your awareness and determination to live in peace and joy. How many days slip by in forgetfulness? What are you doing with your life? Look deeply, and smile. The source of a true smile is an awakened mind.

How can you remember to smile when you wake up? You might hang a reminder—such as a branch, a leaf, a painting, or some inspiring words—in your window or from the ceiling above your bed, so that you notice it when you wake up. Once you develop the practice of smiling, you may not need a sign. You will smile as soon as you hear a bird sing or see the sunlight stream through the window. Smiling helps you approach the day with gentleness and understanding.

The last line of this gatha comes from the "Universal Door" chapter of the *Lotus Sutra*. The one who "looks at all beings with eyes of compassion" is Avalokitesvara, the *bodhisattva* of compassion. In the sutra, this line reads: "Eyes of loving kindness look on all living beings." Love is impossible without understanding. In order to understand others, we must know them, "be inside their skin." Then we can treat them with loving kindness. The source of love is our fully awakened mind.

2. TAKING THE FIRST STEP OF THE DAY

Walking on the Earth
is a miracle!
Each mindful step
reveals the wondrous Dharmakaya.

This poem can be recited as we get out of bed and our feet touch the floor. It can also be used during walking meditation or any time we stand up and walk.

Walking on the Earth is a miracle! We do not have to walk in space or on water to experience a miracle. The real miracle is to be awake in the present moment. Walking on the green Earth, we can realize the wonder of being alive. If we make steps like this, the sun of the *Dharmakaya* will shine.

3. OPENING THE WINDOW

Opening the window,
I look out onto the Dharmakaya.
How wondrous is life!
Attentive to each moment,
my mind is clear like a calm river.

After you wake up, you probably open the curtains and look outside. You may even like to open the window and feel the cool morning air with the dew still on the grass. But is what you see really "outside"? In fact, it is your own mind. As the sun sends its rays through the window, you are not just yourself. You are also the beautiful view from your window. You are the *Dharmakaya*.

Dharmakaya literally means the "body" (*kaya*) of the Buddha's teachings (*Dharma*), the way of understanding and love. Before passing away, the Buddha told his disciples, "Only my physical body will pass away. My Dharma body will remain with you forever." In Mahayana Buddhism, the word has come to mean "the essence of all that exists." All phenomena—the song of a bird, the warm rays of the sun, a cup of hot tea—are manifestations of the Dharmakaya. We, too, are of the same nature as these wonders of the universe.

When we open the window and look out onto the Dharmakaya, we see that life is infinitely marvelous. At that very moment, we can vow to be awake all day long, realizing joy, peace, freedom, and harmony throughout our lives. When we do this, our mind becomes clear like a calm river.

4. LOOKING IN THE MIRROR

Awareness is a mirror
reflecting the four elements.
Beauty is a heart that generates love
and a mind that is open.

The moments during the day of looking in a mirror can be moments of deep awareness. The mirror can serve as a tool for cultivating mindfulness so that we develop a broad capacity to understand and love others. Anyone who maintains awareness in the present moment becomes beautiful and naturally emanates peace, joy, and happiness. A calm half smile and a loving heart are refreshing, and they allow miracles to unfold. The Buddha's smile is beautiful because it expresses tolerance, compassion, and loving kindness.

In traditional cultures, the four great elements were earth, water, fire, and air. The Vietnamese poet Tru Vu wrote:

The flower, whose fragrance is ephemeral,
is made of the four elements.
Your eyes, shining with love,
are also made of the four elements.

The poet is saying that the four elements are neither mind nor matter. They are the universe itself revealed to us. When your mind is the clear mirror of meditative awareness, you will know that you are the outward expression of the essence of reality. So please smile. Smile with your eyes, not just with your lips. Smile with your whole being, reflecting the four elements in the mirror of mindful awareness.

5. USING THE TOILET

Defiled or immaculate,
increasing or decreasing—
these concepts exist only in our minds.
The reality of interbeing is unsurpassed.

Life is always changing. Each thing relies on every other thing for its very existence. If our mind is calm and clear, using the toilet can be as sacred as lighting incense. To accept life is to accept both birth and death, gain and loss, joy and sorrow, defilement and purity. The *Heart Sutra* teaches us that when we see things as they are, we do not discriminate between seeming opposites such as these.

Everything "inter-is." Understanding the truth of nonduality allows us to overcome all pain. Reciting this gatha can help us apply the teachings of the *Heart Sutra*, even during what is usually regarded as a mundane act.

6. TURNING ON THE WATER

Water flows from high in the mountains.
Water runs deep in the Earth.
Miraculously, water comes to us,
and sustains all life.

Even if we know the source of our water, we still take its appearance for granted. But it is thanks to water that life is possible. Our bodies are more than seventy percent water. Our food can be grown and raised because of water. Water is a good friend, a bodhisattva, which nourishes the many thousands of species on Earth. Its benefits are numberless. Reciting this gatha before turning on the faucet or drinking a glass of water enables us to see the stream of fresh water in our own hearts so that we feel completely refreshed. To celebrate the gift of water is to cultivate awareness and help sustain our life and the lives of others.

7. WASHING YOUR HANDS

Water flows over these hands.
May I use them skillfully
to preserve our precious planet.

Our beautiful Earth is endangered. We are about to exhaust her resources by polluting her rivers, lakes, and oceans, thus destroying the habitats of many species, including our own. We are destroying the forests, the ozone layer, and the air. Because of our ignorance, fears, and hatred of one another, our planet may be destroyed as an environment hospitable to human life.

The Earth stores water, and water gives life. Observe your hands as the water runs over them. Do you have enough clear insight to preserve and protect this beautiful planet, our Mother Earth?

8. BRUSHING YOUR TEETH

Brushing my teeth and rinsing my mouth,
I vow to speak purely and lovingly.
When my mouth is fragrant with right speech,
a flower blooms in the garden of my heart.

Each toothpaste manufacturer tells us that his brand will make our mouth clean and our breath fragrant. But if we do not practice "Right Speech," our breath can never be completely fragrant. In Vietnamese we say, "Your words smell bad!" to mean "Your words are not kind or constructive, but rather they are sharp, slanderous, and misleading." Our speech can build a world of peace and joy in which trust and love can flourish, or it can create discord and hatred. "Right Speech" means that our words are both truthful and beautiful.

In 1964, several of us founded a new Buddhist order, the Order of Interbeing. The ninth precept of the Order reads:

Do not say untruthful things for the sake of personal interest or to impress people. Do not utter words that can cause division and hatred. Do not spread news that you do not know to be certain. Do not criticize or condemn things that you are not sure of. Always speak truthfully and constructively. Have the courage to speak out about situations of injustice, even when doing so may threaten your own safety.

When we remember to speak words which are true, kind, and constructive, we nourish a beautiful flower in our hearts, and we can offer its sweet fragrance to everyone.

9. BATHING

Unborn and indestructible,
beyond time and space—
both transmission and inheritance
lie in the wonderful nature of the Dharmadhatu.

Whenever we take a bath or a shower, we can look at our body and see that it is a gift from our parents and their parents. Many of us in the West do not want to have much to do with our parents. They may have hurt us so much. But when we look deeply, we discover that it is impossible to drop all identity with them. As we wash each part of our body, we can meditate on the nature of the body and the nature of consciousness, asking ourselves, "To whom does this body belong? Who has transmitted this body to me? What has been transmitted?"

If we meditate in this way, we will discover that there are three components: the transmitter, that which is transmitted, and the one who receives the transmission. The transmitter is our parents. We are the continuation of our parents and their ancestors. The object of transmission is our body itself, and the one who receives the transmission is us. As we continue to meditate on this, we see clearly that the transmitter, the object transmitted, and the receiver are one. All three are present in our body. When we are deeply in touch with the present moment, we can see that all our ancestors and all future generations are present in us. Seeing this, we will know what to do and what not to do— for ourselves, our ancestors, our children, and their children.

The Dharmadhatu is all that is manifested from the Dharmakaya, having Dharmakaya as its essence, just as all waves are manifestations of water. The Dharmadhatu is neither born nor destroyed. It has no previous existence and no future existence. Its existence is beyond time and space. When we understand this truth of existence with our whole being, we will begin to transcend the fear of death, and we will not be disturbed by unnecessary discriminations.

10. LOOKING AT YOUR HAND

Whose hand is this
that has never died?
Who is it who was born in the past?
Who is it who will die in the future?

If you look deeply into the palm of your hand, you will see your parents and all generations of your ancestors. All of them are alive in this moment.

Each is present in your body. You are the continuation of each of these people.

To be born means that something which did not exist comes into existence. But the day we are "born" is not our beginning. It is a day of continuation. But that should not make us less happy when we celebrate our "Happy Continuation Day."

Since we are never born, how can we cease to be? This is what the *Heart Sutra* reveals to us. When we have a tangible experience of non-birth and non-death, we know ourselves beyond duality. The meditation on "no separate self" is one way to pass through the gate of birth and death.

Your hand proves that you have never been born and you will never die. The thread of life has never been interrupted from time without beginning until now. Previous generations, all the way back to single-celled beings, are present in your hand at this moment. You can observe and experience this. Your hand is always available as a subject for meditation.

11. WASHING YOUR FEET

Peace and joy in each toe—
my own peace and joy.

We take our toes for granted. We worry about so many things, but we seldom think about our toes. If one small toe steps on a thorn, however, our whole body will feel the pain. Holding one toe in our hand, we can feel its peace and joy. It has been a good friend. It is not broken. It does not have cancer. We can thank our toe for its health and well-being. Our toe and each cell of our body exist interdependently, not separately. If our body becomes ill or injured, the cause may be external, such as bacteria from contaminated food, alcohol in another driver's bloodstream, or a bomb dropped from a plane. If the sun were to stop shining, life on earth would cease. We must understand that our body also includes all of these things. The sun is our heart outside of our body. Our life and the life of all existence are one continuous life. The peace and joy of our small toe are the peace and joy of our whole body and mind, and the peace and joy of the entire universe. Once we identify with our toe, we can proceed further to identify ourselves with all life. Life comes from the whole universe. When we identify with the life of all that exists, we realize that birth and death are minor fluctuations in an ever-changing cosmos.

12. GETTING DRESSED

Putting on these clothes,
I am grateful to those who made them
and to the materials from which they were made.
I wish everyone could have enough to wear.

This gatha is an adaptation of a Vietnamese folk song: "My father works the land for the rice we eat. My mother sews the clothes I wear at every season." Today, not many of our fathers work the land; we buy our food in a store. Nor do many of our mothers sew our clothes; we buy manufactured clothes. By introducing the word "grateful," which is not in the folk song, the meaning becomes wider. In Zen monasteries, before eating, the monks reflect on the sources of their food. As we get dressed in the morning, we can contemplate the sources of our clothing and the fact that not everyone has enough to wear.

VERSES FOR MEDITATION

13. INVITING THE BELL TO SOUND

Body, speech, and mind in perfect oneness—
I send my heart along with the sound of the bell.
May the hearers awaken from forgetfulness
and transcend all anxiety and sorrow.

In Buddhist meditation centers, we often use bowl-shaped bells to punctuate the day, calling the community to mindfulness. Standing or sitting in front of the bell, we join our palms, breathe three times, and recite this verse. We hold the bell "inviter" (a wooden stick) in one hand, and the bell, if it is small enough, in the palm of the other, concentrating on the position of our hand and the stick. First we "wake up the bell" by touching its rim lightly with the inviter. This brief sound tells everyone that a full sound of the bell will come in a moment.

During retreats, the sound of the bell reminds us to return to our breathing in the present moment. When we hear it, we stop talking and thinking, and breathe consciously three times. It is important that the person who invites the bell to sound quiets his own being first. If his body, speech, and mind are quiet and in harmony when he invites the bell, the sound will be solid, beautiful, and joyful, and this will help the hearers wake up to the present moment and overcome all anxiety and sorrow.

14. HEARING THE BELL

Listen, listen,
this wonderful sound
brings me back
to my true self.

Listening to the bell, our mind becomes one with the sound as it vibrates along, settles down, and fades away. With the help of the bell, our mind is collected and brought back to the present moment. The bell of mindfulness is the voice of the Buddha calling us back to ourselves. We have to respect each sound, stop our thinking and talking, and get in touch with ourselves, breathing and smiling. This is not a Buddha from the outside. It is our own Buddha calling us home.

If we cannot hear the sound of the bell, then we cannot hear other sounds which also come from the Buddha—the whistling of the wind, the songs of the birds, the cries of a baby, or even the engines of cars. These are all calls from the Buddha, reminding us to return to our "true selves."

What is a "true self"? A true self is a self made of non-self elements. If we are able to look in this way, the word "self" will no longer be a source of confusion. Practicing with a bell helps us practice conscious breathing and realize the interdependent nature of all existence.

15. ENTERING THE MEDITATION ROOM

Entering the meditation room,
I see my true mind.
I vow that once I sit down,
all disturbances will stop.

In Buddhist centers, the most important room is the meditation hall. It is a calm, peaceful place. As we enter, we can stop for a moment, look inside ourselves, and recite this gatha. Then we may like to join our palms and bow quietly as we enter the room.

I think it would be a good idea if each household had a "breathing room." We have so many rooms —for sleeping, eating, and so forth. Why not a room for breathing? Each time we need to return to ourselves, we can go into this simple room and sit quietly, following our breathing. Conscious breathing is very important.

When we sit down in the lotus position or the chrysanthemum position and allow our mind to settle, disturbances diminish, and we feel calm and alert. The "chrysanthemum position" is any position you find comfortable and conducive for meditation. You can sit cross-legged, on your heels, in a chair, or you can even lie down.

In the Vietnamese version of this gatha, the word for "disturbances" is *tram luan*. It means "sinking into and rolling in the ocean of forgetfulness, worries, and afflictions." Stepping into the meditation room, we can remember our desire for complete liberation. By dwelling in the present moment, our steps can establish total freedom so that peace and equanimity are available at once.

16. SITTING DOWN

Sitting here
is like sitting under the Bodhi tree.
My body is mindfulness itself,
entirely free from distraction.

The reason the species *Ficus religiosa* is called the bodhi tree is because the Buddha realized complete awakening at the foot of this kind of tree. *Bodhi* means to be awake or liberated. Today, the place where Buddha realized awakening is called Bodh Gaya, and a large temple has been built there to commemorate his awakening. The bodhi tree stands, beautiful with its luxuriant growth, although it is only a grandchild of the tree which stood there in the Buddha's time.

When we arrive at our meditation cushion or chair, we can join our palms, make a small bow from the waist, and recite this verse. Then we sit down slowly and carefully. When we sit on our cushion with the intention of realizing full awareness of the present moment, our sitting is the continuation of the Buddha's awakened mind. Meditation is not passive sitting in silence. It is sitting in awareness, free from distraction, and realizing the clear understanding that arises from concentration.

17. LIGHTING A CANDLE

Respectful of countless Buddhas,
I calmly light this candle,
brightening the face of the Earth.

In India and other Asian countries, we offer light, sound, smell, and taste to the figures on the altar or shrine. We usually have a candle, some flowers, a bowl of fruit, and a stick of incense. As we light the candle mindfully, the veils of ignorance and forget-fulness naturally dissolve, and the Earth herself becomes light.

There is a story in the life of the Buddha which describes how profound an offering of light can be. One day, the King, Queen, and people of the city of Sravasti wanted to honor the Buddha by lighting thousands of lamps around the Jetavana mona-stery. An old mendicant woman wanted to make an offering, but after a whole day of begging, she only had one cent. So she decided not to eat, and she bought some oil with the penny and poured it into one of the many lamps exhibited at the gate of the monastery. Early in the morning, the Venera-ble Maha Maudgalyayana went out to blow out the lamps. All the lamps went out except the one with the oil poured by the beggar woman. As he tried again and again to blow it out, it only grew brighter and brighter. A candle offered in mindfulness will give no less light than the oil lamp the old beggar woman offered Buddha many years ago.

Although this gatha was composed for lighting a candle in the meditation hall, it can be used when we light candles anywhere, such as during a vigil for human rights. It can even be used along with the gatha for turning on an electric light.

18. OFFERING INCENSE

In gratitude, we offer this incense
to all Buddhas and bodhisattvas
throughout space and time.
May it be fragrant as Earth herself,
reflecting our careful efforts,
our wholehearted awareness,
and the fruit of understanding, slowly ripening.
May we be companions of Buddhas and bodhisattvas.
May we awaken from forgetfulness
and realize our true home.

In Vietnamese Zen temples, we say this gatha silently as we offer incense alone, or aloud when we conduct ceremonies with others. As we say it, we imagine fragrant smoke rising in the air, becoming a cloud of five colors. This represents the offering to all Buddhas throughout space and time, of the five-fold fragrance–precepts, concentration, understanding, liberation, and insight. We call it the "fragrance of the heart," a delight which is available to us every day, although not for sale in stores.

Since liberation and insight all arise from awakened understanding, we refer only to three of the fragrances in this gatha: our careful efforts (the precepts), our wholehearted awareness (concentration), and the fruit of our understanding. Full awareness comes from carefully keeping the precepts, and understanding comes from full awareness.

When we offer incense, we vow with all beings to leave the world of forgetfulness and return to the world of awakening. Forgetfulness is the lack of mindfulness. Awakening is true freedom.

19. PRAISING BUDDHA

As refreshing as a lotus flower,
as bright as the North Star:
to the Buddha, I go for refuge.

In my tradition, we join our palms together before the image of the Buddha, our teacher, and praise his beauty which is the fruit of love and understanding. Lotus flowers are fresh and pure, and they can be compared with love. The North Star helps travelers find their direction, so it symbolizes understanding. To take refuge in the Buddha is to seek protection in understanding, loving kindness, and compassion.

20. FINDING A STABLE SITTING POSITION

In the lotus position,
the human flower blooms.
The udumbara flower is present,
giving forth its fragrance.

When you sit down to meditate, try to find a stable, comfortable posture. The half-lotus and full-lotus positions are excellent for establishing stability of body and mind. Choose a cushion which is the right thickness to support you. Allow your back to be straight, keep your eyes half closed, and fold your hands comfortably on your lap. If you prefer, find a good position sitting in a chair or lying on the floor.

In Buddhist mythology, the udumbara flower (*Ficus glomerata*) blooms once every 3,000 years. To see a fully awakened person, a Buddha, is so rare that it is like seeing an udumbara flower. In the Tu Hiêu Monastery in Hue, there is a scroll which says: "The udumbara flower, although fallen from the stem, is still fragrant." Just as the fragrance of the udumbara flower cannot be destroyed, our capacity for enlightenment is always present. The Buddha taught that everyone is a Buddha, everyone is an udumbara flower. Dwelling in mindfulness, we allow the lovely, healing fragrance of the udumbara flower to permeate our lives.

21. ADJUSTING MEDITATION POSTURE

Feelings come and go
like clouds in a windy sky.
Conscious breathing
is my anchor.

If your legs or feet fall asleep or begin to hurt during sitting meditation so that your concentration becomes disturbed, feel free to adjust your position. If you are sitting in the half-lotus position, you can put the foot which is resting on top of your thigh underneath it. If you are sitting in the full-lotus, you can change the foot you placed first with the foot you placed second. If you do this slowly and attentively, following your breathing and each movement, you will not lose a single moment of concentration. If the pain is severe, stand up, walk slowly and mindfully, and then when you are ready, sit down again.

In some meditation centers, practitioners are not permitted to move during sitting meditation. They often have to endure great discomfort. To me, this seems unnatural. When a part of our body is numb or in pain, it is telling us something, and we should listen to it. Sitting in meditation is to cultivate peace and joy, not to endure physical strain. To change the position of our feet or do a little walking meditation will not disturb others very much, and it can help us a lot. This gatha is for you to recite when you change the position of your legs.

According to the *Abhidharma* texts of Buddhist psychology, there are three types of feelings—pleasant, unpleasant, and neutral. This way of dividing the feelings does not seem to me to be very accurate. According to my experience, when there is awareness, neutral feelings can become very pleasant feelings, which are more sound and longer lasting than even the other categories of pleasant feelings.

To eat good food or hear words of praise usually gives rise to a pleasant feeling. Flying into a rage or having a toothache is an unpleasant feeling. These feelings usually push us around, and we become like clouds blown in the wind. Our feelings of peace and joy will be more stable and lasting if we know the source of our so-called neutral feelings. The essence of happiness is a body which is not in pain and a heart and mind which are not oppressed by anxiety, fear, or hatred. Sitting in meditation, we can arrive at a stable feeling of joy, realizing the stillness of body and the clarity of mind. We are no longer pushed around by these "roots of affliction," (Sanskrit: *klesha*) and we experience a feeling of well-being. The necessary condition for the existence of peace and joy is the awareness that peace and joy are available.

We have eyes which can perceive the forms of so many flowers and trees. If we are aware that our eyes and the forms they behold are precious, the feeling we have when we see these forms will be pleasant. Without this awareness, the feeling will be "neutral." It depends on us.

Sitting meditation is to establish stillness, peace, and joy. Just as an anchor holds a boat so that it does not drift away, conscious breathing sustains our awareness of the present moment, and keeps us in touch with our true selves.

22. OPENING THE SUTRA

The Dharma is deep and lovely.
We now have a chance to see it,
study it, and practice it.
I vow to realize its true meaning.

In the temple, we chant this gatha before studying or reciting the sutras, which are the words of the Buddha. Reciting sutras with respect and sincerity enables us to understand them. Otherwise, even if we enter the ocean of great understanding, we will return empty-handed without a single pearl.

This gatha encourages us to prepare ourselves to receive the teachings and practice them in our own lives.

23. CLOSING THE SUTRA

Reciting the sutras, practicing the way of awareness,
gives rise to benefits without limit.
I vow to share the fruits with all beings.
I vow to offer tribute to parents, teachers,
friends, and numerous beings
who give guidance and support along the path.

In the temple, we chant this gatha after reciting sutras or precepts. Regular recitation of sutras and precepts can give rise to deep understanding. When we understand the words and put them into practice, we can find our own path and help show the way for others.

In the Four Great Vows recited at Zen temples, we say "Sentient being are numberless, I vow to save them all" or "I vow to transport all sentient beings to the other shore," the shore of liberation. The line "I vow to offer tribute to parents, teachers, friends, and numerous beings" replaces "I vow to transport all sentient beings to the other shore." It has a wider meaning and is more approachable than the traditional way of offering merit. We offer tribute to the parents who gave us birth and raised us; to the teachers who have instructed us; to the friends who have supported us in difficult times; and to all species of beings with whom we are interrelated and interdependent. It is the same as vowing to bring all sentient beings to the other shore, but simpler and more practical.

24. FOLLOWING THE BREATH

Breathing in, I calm my body.
Breathing out, I smile.
Dwelling in the present moment,
I know this is a wonderful moment!

In our busy society, it is a great fortune to be able to breathe consciously from time to time. Our body and mind become calm and concentrated, bringing us joy, peace, and ease. We can breathe consciously while sitting in meditation or anytime throughout the day. While breathing, we can recite this gatha. "Breathing in, I calm my body." This line is like drinking a glass of cold water. You feel the cool freshness permeating your body. When I breathe in and recite this line, I actually feel the breathing calming my body and mind. "Breathing out, I smile." A smile can relax hundreds of muscles in your face, and make you master of yourself. That is why the Buddhas and bodhisattvas are always smiling.

"Dwelling in the present moment." While I sit here, I don't think of anything else. I sit here, and I know where I am. "I know this is a wonderful moment." It is a joy to sit, stable and at ease, and re-turn to ourselves—our breathing, our half smile, our true nature. We can appreciate these moments. We can ask ourselves, "If I do not have peace and joy right now, when will I have peace and joy—tomorrow or after tomorrow? What is preventing me from being happy right now?" When we fol-low our breathing, we can say "calming, smiling, present moment, wonderful moment."

This exercise is not just for beginners. Many of us who have practiced for forty or fifty years con-tinue to practice in the same way, because it is so vital. In *The Sutra on the Full Awareness of Breathing*

(Anapanasati), the Buddha proposed sixteen exercises to help us breathe consciously. This gatha is a condensation of many of these exercises. Another condensation is this verse:

> *Breathing in, I know I'm breathing in.*
> *Breathing out, I know*
> *as the in-breath grows deep,*
> *the out-breath grows slow.*
> *Breathing in makes me calm.*
> *Breathing out brings me ease.*
> *With the in-breath, I smile.*
> *With the out-breath, I release.*
> *Breathing in, there is only the present moment.*
> *Breathing out, it is a wonderful moment.*

The verse can be summarized in these eight words and two phrases:

> *In, Out; Deep, Slow;*
> *Calm, Ease; Smile, Release;*
> *Present Moment, Wonderful Moment.*

This is very easy to practice—while sitting, walking, standing, or doing any activity.

First, we practice "In, Out." Breathing in, we say, "In," silently, in order to nourish the awareness that we are breathing in. When we breathe out, we say, "Out," aware that we are breathing out. Each word is a guide to help us return to our breathing in the present moment. We can repeat "In, Out" until we find that our concentration is peaceful and solid. Most important is that we enjoy doing it. Then we say "Deep" with the next inhalation, and "Slow" with our exhalation. When we breathe consciously, our breathing becomes deeper and slower. We do not have to make a special effort, but only notice that it is deeper and slower, more peaceful and pleasant. We can continue to breathe, "Deep, Slow, Deep, Slow," until we want to move to the next phrase, which is "Calm, Ease."

The word "Calm" comes from the exercise in the *Sutra* which is, "I am breathing in and making the activities of my whole body calm and at peace. I am breathing out and making the activities of my whole body calm and at peace." The word "body" here also means "mind," because during the practice, body and mind become one.

When we breathe out, we say, "Ease." Ease means a feeling of not being pressured, feeling free. Our time is only for breathing and enjoying breathing. We feel light and free, at ease. We know that breathing is the most important thing at this moment, so we just enjoy the practice of breathing. The feeling of ease is one of the seven factors of enlightenment in Buddhism.

When we have mastered "Calm, Ease," we move to "Smile, Release." When we breathe in, even if we do not feel great joy at that moment, we can still smile. But in fact it is unlikely, because after practicing breathing in this way, we already have joy and peace. When we smile, our joy and peace become even more settled, and tension vanishes. It is a kind of "mouth yoga." We smile for everyone.

When we breathe out, we say "Release." Everyone has pain and suffering. We have to be able to let go of them and to smile at our suffering. We can only do this if we know that the present moment is the only moment in which we can be alive. "Present Moment, Wonderful Moment." How wonderful to be alive!

25. HUGGING MEDITATION

Breathing in, I am so happy to hug my child.
Breathing out, I know she is real and alive in my arms.

Suppose a lovely child comes and presents herself to us. If we are not really there—if we are thinking of the past, worrying about the future, or possessed by anger or fear—the child, although present, will not exist for us. She is like a ghost, and we are like a ghost also. If we want to meet the child, we have to go back to the present moment in order to meet her. If we want to hug her, it is in the present moment that we can hug her.

So we breathe consciously, uniting body and mind, making ourselves into a real person again. When we become a real person, the child becomes real also. She is a wondrous presence and the encounter with life is possible at that moment. If we hold her in our arms and continue to breathe, life is. This gatha can help us remember the preciousness of our loved one as we hold him or her in our arms.

26. GREETING SOMEONE

A lotus for you,
a Buddha to be.

The tradition of joining our palms together and bowing when we meet someone is very beautiful. Millions of men and women in Asia greet each other this way every day. When someone offers me a cup of tea, I always bow respectfully. As I join my palms, I breathe in and say, "A lotus for you." As I bow, I breathe out and say, "A Buddha to be." To join our palms in a lotus bud is to offer the person standing before us a fresh flower. But we have to remember not to join our palms mechanically. We must be aware of the person we are greeting. When our respect is sincere, we remember that he or she has the nature of a Buddha, the nature of awakening.

It is necessary for us to see the Buddha in the person before us. If we practice this way regularly, we will see a change in ourselves. We will develop humility, and we will also realize that our abilities are boundless. When we know how to respect others, we also know how to respect ourselves.

As I bow, mindfulness becomes real in me. Seeing my deep reverence, the person to whom I bow also becomes awake, and he or she may like to form a lotus and bow to me, breathing in and out. With one greeting, mindfulness becomes present in both of us as we touch the Buddha with our hearts, not just with our hands. Suddenly, the Buddha in each of us begins to shine, and we are in touch with the present moment.

Sometimes we think that we are superior to others—perhaps more educated or intelligent. Seeing an uneducated person, a feeling of disdain may arise, but this attitude does not help anyone. Our knowledge is relative and limited. An orchid, for example, knows how to produce noble, symmetrical flowers, and a snail knows how to make a beautiful, well-proportioned shell. Compared with this kind of knowledge, our knowledge is not worth boasting about, even if we have a Ph.D. We should bow deeply before the orchid and the snail and join our palms reverently before the monarch butterfly and the magnolia tree. Feeling respect for all species of living beings and inanimate objects will help us recognize a part of the Buddha nature in ourselves.

In the West, you may prefer to shake hands. But if you greet others mindfully and respectfully, whatever form you use, the Buddha is present. Forming a lotus bud with your hands is very pleasant. I hope you will try it from time to time. If a tulip blossom is more familiar for you to envision, you may want to say, "A tulip for you, a Buddha to be." A tulip possesses the Buddha nature just like a lotus.

27. CLEANING THE MEDITATION ROOM

As I clean this fresh, calm room,
boundless joy and energy arise!

It is a joy to tidy the meditation room. In its fresh, calm atmosphere, everything reminds us to come back to the present moment. Every sweep of the broom is light, and every step we take is filled with awareness. As we arrange the cushions, our mind is still. Working in a relaxed way, with a feeling of peace and joy, we become energized. Everything we do can be filled with this peace and joy.

28. SWEEPING

As I carefully sweep the ground of enlightenment,
a tree of understanding springs up from the Earth.

This gatha is based on two lines of Chinese poetry: "Sweeping the floor of the monastery, the benefits of understanding are realized." The monastery is the land of the Buddha. The path around our home is also the ground of awakening.

It is said that Mara, who represents delusion, offered the Buddha a parcel of land as large as the Buddha's robe could cover. But when the Buddha's robe flew up to the sky and covered the entire Earth with its shadow, Mara was surprised. So we say that the Earth on which we stand, the earth in front of our house, and the earth which we cultivate, all belong to the Buddha. In Vietnam, at the New Year (Tết), we put poles in front of our houses to remind Mara how far Buddha's land extends— and to keep Mara out!

Any ground we sweep in full awareness is the ground of enlightenment. True meditation always gives rise to awakened understanding.

29. CLEANING THE BATHROOM

How wonderful it is to scrub and clean.
Day by day, the heart and mind grow clearer.

Most of us do not like cleaning the bathroom. But when we work in full awareness of the present moment, we can find purity in each act. To purify means to become clear and calm. Cleaning the bathroom, we clear and purify our environment and ourselves.

In centers for meditation practice, often there is a vase of flowers in every bathroom. The bathroom is as important a place as the meditation hall for practicing mindfulness. In fact, the bathroom is another meditation hall, and so we offer a vase of flowers there. Flowers arranged with skill and care remind us that we can live in such a way to clarify and calm our hearts and minds. I hope you will put a vase of flowers in your bathroom at home.

VERSES FOR EATING MINDFULLY

A few years ago, I asked some children, "What is the purpose of eating breakfast?" One boy replied, "To get energy for the day." Another said, "The purpose of eating breakfast is to eat breakfast." I think the second child is more correct. The purpose of eating is to eat.

Eating a meal in mindfulness is an important practice. We turn off the TV, put down our newspaper, and work together for five or ten minutes, setting the table and finishing whatever needs to be done. During these few minutes, we can be very happy. When the food is on the table and everyone is seated (remember the gatha for sitting down), we practice breathing: "Breathing in, I calm my body. Breathing out, I smile," three times. We can recover ourselves completely after three breaths like this.

Then, we look at each person as we breathe in and out in order to be in touch with ourselves and everyone at the table. We don't need two hours in order to see another person. If we are really settled within ourselves, we only need to look for one or two seconds, and that is enough to see our friend. I think that if a family has five members, only about five or ten seconds is needed to practice this "looking and seeing."

After breathing, we smile. Sitting at the table with other people, we have a chance to offer an authentic smile of friendship and understanding. It is very easy, but not many people do it. To me, this is the most important practice. We look at each person and smile at him or her. Breathing and smiling together are very important practices. If the people in a family cannot smile at each other, the situation is a very dangerous one.

After breathing and smiling, we look down at the food in a way that allows the food to become real. This food reveals our connection with the Earth. Each bite contains the life of the sun and the Earth. The extent to which our food reveals itself depends on us. We can see and taste the whole universe in a piece of bread! Contemplating our food for a few seconds before eating, and eating in mindfulness, can bring us much happiness.

Having the opportunity to sit with our family and friends and enjoy wonderful food is something precious, something not everyone has. Many people in the world are hungry. When I hold a bowl of rice or a piece of bread, I know that I am fortunate, and I feel compassion for all those who have no food to eat and are without friends or family. This is a very deep practice. We do not need to go to a temple or a church in order to practice this. We can practice it right at our dinner table. Mindful eating can cultivate seeds of compassion and understanding that will strengthen us to do something to help hungry and lonely people be nourished.

In order to aid mindfulness during meals, you may like to eat silently from time to time. Your first silent meal may cause you to feel a little uncomfortable, but once you become used to it, you will realize that meals in silence bring much peace and happiness. It is like turning off the TV before eating. We "turn off" the talking in order to enjoy the food and the presence of one another.

I do not recommend silent meals every day. I think talking to each other is a wonderful way to be in touch. But we have to distinguish among different kinds of talk. Some subjects can separate us, for instance if we talk about other people's shortcomings. The food that has been prepared carefully will have no value if we let this kind of talk dominate our meal. When instead we speak about things that nourish our awareness of the food and our being together, we cultivate the kind of happiness that is necessary for us to grow. If we compare this experience with the experience of talking about other people's shortcomings, I think awareness of a piece of bread in your mouth is a much more nourishing experience. It brings life in and makes life real.

I propose that during eating, you refrain from discussing subjects which can destroy the awareness of the family and the food. But you should feel free to say things that can nourish awareness and happiness. For instance, if there is a dish that you like very much, you can see if other people are also enjoying it, and if one of them is not, you can help him or her appreciate the wonderful dish prepared with loving care. If someone is thinking about something other than the good food on the table, such as his difficulties in the office or with friends, it means he is losing the present moment, and the food. You can say, "This dish is wonderful, don't you agree?" When you say something like this, you will draw him out of his thinking and worries, and bring him back to the here and now, enjoying you, enjoying the wonderful dish. You become a bodhisattva, helping a living being become enlightened. I know that children, in particular, are very capable of practicing mindfulness and reminding others to do the same.

The verses which follow can help us practice mindfulness while eating.

30. LOOKING AT YOUR EMPTY PLATE

My plate, empty now,
will soon be filled
with precious food.

I am aware that when many people on this Earth look at an empty plate, their plate will continue to be empty for a long time. I am grateful to have food to eat, and I vow to find ways to help those who are hungry.

31. SERVING FOOD

In this food,
I see clearly the presence
of the entire universe
supporting my existence.

This verse helps us see the principle of dependent co-arising, as we see that our life and the lives of all species are inter-related.

32. CONTEMPLATING YOUR FOOD

This plate of food,.
so fragrant and appetizing,
also contains much suffering.

This gatha has its roots in a Vietnamese folk song. When we look at our plate, filled with fragrant and appetizing food, we should be aware of the bitter pain of people who suffer from hunger. Every day, 40,000 children die as a result of hunger and malnutrition. Every day! Such a figure shocks us every time we hear it. Looking at our plate, we can "see" Mother Earth, the farm workers, and the tragedy of hunger and malnutrition.

We who live in North America and Europe are accustomed to eating grains and other foods imported from the Third World such as coffee from Colombia, chocolate from Ghana, or fragrant rice from Thailand. We must be aware that children in these countries, except those from rich families, never see such fine products. They eat inferior foods, while the finer products we eat are put aside for export in order to bring in foreign exchange. There are even some parents who, because they do not have the means to feed their children, resort to selling their children to be servants to families who have enough to eat.

Before a meal, we can join our palms in mindfulness and think about the children who do not have enough to eat. Slowly and mindfully we breathe three times and recite this gatha. Doing so will help us maintain mindfulness. Perhaps one day we will find ways to live more simply in order to have more time and energy to do something to change the system of injustice which exists in the world.

33. BEGINNING TO EAT

With the first taste, I promise to offer joy.
With the second, I promise to help relieve the suffering of others.
With the third, I promise to see others' joy as my own.
With the fourth, I promise to learn the way of non-attachment and equanimity.

This verse reminds us of the Four Immeasurables (Sanskrit: *Brahmaviharas*)—loving kindness, compassion, sympathetic joy, and non-attachment. These are said to be the four abodes of the Buddhas and bodhisattvas. During the time we eat the first mouthful, we may like to express our gratitude by promising to bring joy to at least one person. With the second mouthful, we can promise to help relieve the pain of at least one person. After the fourth mouthful, we get in touch with the food and its deep nature.

34. FINISHING YOUR MEAL

The plate is empty.
My hunger is satisfied.
I vow to live
for the benefit of all beings.

This verse reminds us of the Four Gratitudes—to parents, teachers, friends, and all organic and inorganic species that support and enrich our lives.

35. WASHING THE DISHES

Washing the dishes
is like bathing a baby Buddha.
The profane is the sacred.
Everyday mind is Buddha's mind.

To my mind, the idea that doing dishes is unpleasant can occur to us only when we are not doing them. Once we are standing in front of the sink with our sleeves rolled up and our hands in warm water, it is really not bad at all. I enjoy taking my time with each dish, being fully aware of the dish, the water, and each movement of my hands. I know that if I hurry in order to go and have dessert, the time will be unpleasant, not worth living. That would be a pity, for every second of life is a miracle. The dishes themselves and the fact that I am here washing them are miracles!

Each thought, each action in the sunlight of awareness becomes sacred. In this light, no boundary exists between the sacred and the profane. It may take a bit longer to do the dishes, but we can live fully, happily, in every moment. Washing the dishes is at the same time a means and an end— that is, not only do we do the dishes in order to have clean dishes, we also do the dishes just to do the dishes and live fully each moment while washing them.

If I am incapable of washing dishes joyfully, if I want to finish them quickly so I can go and have dessert and a cup of tea, I will be equally incapable of doing these things joyfully. With the cup in my hands, I will be thinking about what to do next, and the fragrance and the flavor of the tea, together with the pleasure of drinking it, will be lost. I will always be dragged into the future, never able to live in the present moment. The time of dishwashing is as important as the time of meditation. That is why the everyday mind is called the Buddha's mind.

36. DRINKING TEA

This cup of tea in my two hands—
mindfulness is held uprightly!
My mind and body dwell
in the very here and now.

Whether you are in a tea meditation ceremony or drinking a cup of tea alone at home or in a café, it is wonderful to allow enough time to appreciate the tea. If the weather is cold, you can feel the warmth of the cup in your hands. In cafés, there are many distractions—music, talking, our own thinking. In that kind of environment, a cup of tea is not very real.

We may need to organize a tea meditation in order to learn the art of drinking tea in mindfulness. Holding a cup of tea in your two hands, breathe consciously, and say the above gatha. Breathe in and recite the first line, breathe out and recite the second. The next inhalation is for the third line, and the exhalation is for the fourth. Breathing mindfully in this way, we recuperate ourselves and the cup of tea reclaims its highest place. If we are not mindful, it is not tea that we are drinking but our own illusions and afflictions.

Often in daily life, our body and mind may not be together. Sometimes our body is here but our mind is lost in the past or in the future. We may be possessed by anger, hatred, jealousy, or anxiety. If we practice the teaching of the Buddha on how to breathe mindfully, we bring mind and body together, and they become one again. This is what is meant by the expression, "oneness of body and mind."

When our mind and body have become one and we are awake, we are ourselves, and we can encounter the tea. If the tea becomes real, we become real. When we are able to truly meet the tea, at that very moment, life is. As we drink the tea, we are well aware that we are drinking the tea. Drinking tea becomes the most important thing in life at that moment. This is the practice of mindfulness.

VERSES FOR OTHER DAILY ACTIVITIES

37. WALKING MEDITATION

The mind can go in a thousand directions.
But on this beautiful path, I walk in peace.
With each step, a gentle wind blows.
With each step, a flower blooms.

Walking meditation can be very enjoyable. We walk slowly, alone or with friends, if possible in some beautiful place. Walking meditation is really to enjoy the walking—walking not in order to arrive, just for walking. The purpose is to be in the present moment and enjoy each step you make. Therefore you have to shake off all worries and anxieties, not thinking of the future, not thinking of the past, just enjoying the present moment. You can take the hand of a child as you walk, as if you are the happiest person on Earth. We walk all the time, but usually it is more like running. Our hurried steps print anxiety and sorrow on the Earth. If we can take one step in peace, we can take two, three, four, and then five steps for the peace and happiness of humankind.

Our mind darts from one thing to another, like a monkey swinging from branch to branch without stopping to rest. Thoughts have millions of pathways, and we are forever pulled along them into the world of forgetfulness. If we can transform our walking path into a field for meditation, our feet will take every step in full awareness. Our breathing will be in harmony with our steps, and our mind will naturally be at ease. Every step we take will reinforce our peace and joy and cause a stream of calm energy to flow through us. Then we can say, "With each step, a gentle wind blows."

The Buddha is often represented by artists as seated upon a lotus flower to suggest the peace and happiness he enjoys. Artists also depict lotus flowers blooming under the footsteps of the newly-born Buddha. If we take steps without anxiety, in peace and joy, then we, too, will cause a flower to bloom on the Earth with every step.

38. GARDENING

Earth brings us into life
and nourishes us.
Earth takes us back again.
Birth and death are present in every moment.

The Earth is our mother. All life arises from her and is nourished by her. Each of us is a child of the Earth and, at some time, the Earth will take us back to her again. In fact, we are continuously coming to life and returning to the bosom of the Earth. We who practice meditation should be able to see birth and death in every breath.

Gardening is a wonderful, restorative activity. If you live in a city, you may not have many opportunities to hoe the earth, plant vegetables, or take care of flowers. That is a pity. Being in touch with Mother Earth is a wonderful way to preserve your mental health.

39. PLANTING TREES OR OTHER PLANTS

I entrust myself to Earth;
Earth entrusts herself to me.
I entrust myself to Buddha;
Buddha entrusts herself to me.

To plant a seed or a seedling is to entrust it to the Earth. The plant takes refuge in the Earth. Whether the plant grows well or not, depends on the Earth. Many generations of vegetation have grown bright and beautiful under the light of the sun to create a fertile topsoil. This topsoil will continue to nourish generations of vegetation to come. Whether the Earth is beautiful, fresh, and green, or withered and dry depends on the plants entrusted to the Earth. The plants and the Earth rely on each other for life.

When we entrust ourselves to the Buddha, we take refuge in the essence of nourishment, the soil of enlightened understanding, love, and compassion. And the Buddha also entrusts herself to us, because awakened understanding, love, and compassion need each of us in order to germinate and flourish. How can these attributes continue to flower in the world if we do not realize them within ourselves? "I entrust myself to the Buddha" is what we usually think, but let us also notice that Buddha is entrusting herself to become real within us, just as the Earth and the green plants entrust themselves to one another.

40. WATERING THE GARDEN

Water and sun
green these plants.
When the rain of compassion falls,
even a desert becomes an immense, green ocean.

Water is the balm, or nurturance, of compassion which has the capacity to restore us to life. The Bodhisattva of Compassion is often depicted holding a vase of water in her left hand, and a willow branch in her right. She sprinkles down compassion, like drops of nurturing balm, to revitalize tired hearts and minds weak from suffering. Rain enlivens crops and protects people from hunger. Watering the garden, the compassionate rain falls on the plants. Our respect and gratitude for this gift of water helps us heal ourselves and transform even a desert into an immense, green ocean.

When we offer water to plants, we offer it to the whole Earth. When watering plants, if we speak to them, we are also speaking to ourselves. We exist in relationship to all other phenomena. As we water plants, we can speak to them:

Dear plant, you are not alone.
This stream of water comes from Earth and sky.
We are together for innumerable lifetimes.

The feeling of alienation among so many people today has come about because they lack awareness of the interconnectedness of all things. We cannot separate ourselves from society or anything else. "This is like this, because that is like that" is a phrase taken from the sutras, summarizing the principle of interrelatedness. To water plants and experience compassion and interconnectedness is a wonderful practice of meditation.

41. CUTTING A FLOWER

May I cut you, little flower,
gift of Earth and sky?
Thank you, dear bodhisattva,
for making life beautiful.

Whenever we cut a flower, we ask permission, not only of the plant, but of the Earth and sky as well. The whole Earth and sky joined to create this flower. Our gratitude to them must be sincere. A flower is a bodhisattva that makes life fresher and more beautiful. We, too, can offer others a gift by being refreshing, compassionate, and happy.

There is a well-known story in Zen circles about a flower. One day the Buddha was holding up a flower in front of an audience of 1,250 monks and nuns. He did not say anything for a long time. A man in the audience, named Mahakasyapa, smiled at him and at the flower. The Buddha smiled back and said, "I have a treasure of insight, and I have

transmitted it to Mahakasyapa." To me the meaning is quite simple: Be in touch with life in the present moment and look deeply into things that
happen in the present moment. The person who
was not thinking, who was just himself, encoun-
tered the flower in depth and smiled.

42. ARRANGING FLOWERS

Arranging this flower
in the Saha World,
the ground of my mind
is pure and calm.

The *Saha* world, according to Buddhist mythology,
is the planet Earth, the "ground" for enduring
hardships, sickness, hatred, ignorance, and war.
Saha means "moving" and "enduring." When we
practice the teachings of the Buddha, we transform
ourselves and set up a beautiful Pure Land, full of
miraculous wonders, here on Earth.

Arranging flowers is something we can do to
help make life more beautiful. When we are mindful while arranging flowers, not only the flowers
become beautiful, but we become beautiful as well.
When our heart's garden is calm and radiant, and
the flowers of our heart light the way, people
around us will recognize the beauty of life and realize how precious it is to be alive.

43. WASHING VEGETABLES

In these fresh vegetables
I see a green sun.
All dharmas join together
to make life possible.

The first two lines are taken from the poem, "Armfuls of Poetry and Bushels of Sunshine" by the author. In fact, it is the sun which is green and not the vegetables, because the green color in the leaves of the vegetables is due to the presence of the sun. Without the sun, no species of living being could survive. Leaves absorb sunlight as it is reflected on their surfaces, and they retain the energy of the sun, extracting the carbon in the atmosphere which manufactures the nutritive matter necessary for the plant.

Therefore, when we see fresh vegetables, we can see the sun in them—a sun green in color—and not just the sun, but thousands of other phenomena as well. For example, if there were no clouds there would be no rain water. Without water, air, and soil, there would be no vegetables. The vegetables are the coming together of many conditions far and near.

In the gatha, the word "dharmas" means phenomena. In everyday life, whenever you are in contact with any phenomenon whatsoever, you can always engage in the practice of meditation on interdependent origination, not just when you are washing vegetables. The Sanskrit word *pratitya-*

samutpada, usually translated "co-dependent origination," means that phenomena exist in relationship to all other things. All dharmas join together, making life possible.

44. THROWING OUT THE GARBAGE

In the garbage I see a rose.
In the rose, I see the garbage.
Everything is in transformation.
Even permanence is impermanent.

Garbage can smell terrible, especially rotting organic matter. But it can also become rich compost for fertilizing the garden. The fragrant rose and the stinking garbage are two sides of the same existence. Without one, the other cannot be. Everything is in transformation. The rose that wilts after six days will become a part of the garbage. After six months the garbage is transformed into a rose. When we speak of impermanence, we understand that everything is in transformation. This becomes that, and that becomes this.

Looking deeply, we can contemplate one thing and see everything else in it. We are not disturbed by change when we see the interconnectedness and continuity of all things. It is not that the life of any individual is permanent, but that life itself continues. When we identify ourselves with life and go beyond the boundaries of a separate identity, we shall be able to see permanence in the impermanent, or the rose in the garbage.

45. SMILING AT YOUR ANGER

Breathing in, I know that anger makes me ugly.
Breathing out, I do not want to be contorted by
anger.
Breathing in, I know I must take care of myself.
Breathing out, I know loving kindness is the only
answer.

When we feel angry, we should go back to our conscious breathing and refrain from looking and listening to the person we think to be the source of our unhappiness. We do not need to do or say anything. As we go back to our breathing and breathe according to the gatha, we should be aware that it is our anger that is making us suffer, not the other person.

Taking the first breath and reciting the first line of the gatha is like looking at ourselves in a mirror. As we see ourselves clearly, we know what to do and what not to do. The exhalation that follows will have the same effect. In anger, we tend to think of the other person as the source of our suffering. We see evil in him or her. "He is cruel." "She oppresses me." "He wants to destroy me!" In fact, it is our anger that destroys us.

So we must take good care of our anger. When a house is burning, we must first go into the house and try to put out the fire. It is too soon to go searching for the person who may have started the fire. That is what we see in the inhalation that goes with the third line of the gatha. When we exhale, we recite the last line. Only loving kindness can take care of our anger, and only loving kindness can take care of the other person.

When we meditate, we learn that understanding is the essence of love and forgiveness. A person who is not happy will do or say things that make other people unhappy. If we are refreshed with the nectar of compassion, we feel a source of well being within ourselves. This happiness will benefit other people. The person we despise needs our compassion, not our hatred, because he or she is so unhappy.

We need to make an effort to smile as we recite the last line of this gatha. This smile will relax our face. Then we can open the door and go outside to practice walking meditation, using the same gatha or any gatha for breathing. The fresh air and the freshness of the outdoors will help us a lot. We should be sure that we are smiling naturally and easily before we return indoors. When we are smiling, we know that our anger has been transformed into understanding and forgiveness.

46. USING THE TELEPHONE

Words can travel thousands of miles.
May my words create mutual understanding and love.
May they be as beautiful as gems,
as lovely as flowers.

The telephone is a very convenient means of communication. It can save us travel time and expense. But the telephone can also tyrannize us. If it is always ringing, we are disturbed and cannot accomplish much. If we talk on the phone without awareness, we waste precious time and money. Often we say things that are not important. How many times have we received our telephone bill and winced at the amount that is due!

When the telephone rings, the bell creates in us a kind of vibration, maybe some anxiety: "Who is calling? Is it good news or bad news?" There is a force which pulls us to the phone. We cannot resist. We are victims of our own telephone.

The next time you hear the phone ring, I recommend that you stay exactly where you are, and become aware of your breathing: "Breathing in, I calm my body. Breathing out, I smile." When the phone rings the second time, you can breathe again. I am sure that this time your smile will be more solid than before. When it rings the third time, you can continue practicing breathing, while moving slowly to the phone. You are your own master, walking like a Buddha to the phone, dwelling in mindfulness. When you pick up the phone, you know that you are smiling, not only for your own sake, but also for the sake of the other person. If you are irritated or angry, the other person will receive your negativity. But since you are smiling, how fortunate for him or her!

You can write down the telephone gatha and tape it onto your phone. I suggest that before you lift the receiver to make a call, you touch the phone, breathe in and out twice, and recite the four lines. Then pick up the phone and dial. When the bell rings, you know that your friend is breathing and smiling and will not pick up the phone until the third ring. So you continue to practice: "Breathing in, I calm my body. Breathing out, I smile." Both of you are close to your phones, breathing and smiling. This is very beautiful! You do not have to go into a meditation hall to do this wonderful practice. It is available in your house or office. Practicing telephone meditation can counteract stress and depression and bring the Buddha into your daily life.

We should not underestimate the effect our words have when we use right speech. The words we speak can build up understanding and love. They can be as beautiful as gems, as lovely as flowers, and they can make many people happy. The telephone gatha can help us practice right speech, and it can also help us keep our phone bills down.

47. TURNING ON THE TELEVISION

The mind is a television
with thousands of channels.
I choose a world that is tranquil and calm
so that my joy will always be fresh.

Mind is consciousness. Consciousness includes the subject which knows and the object which is known. The two aspects, subject and object, depend on each other in order to exist. As the Vietnamese meditation master, Huong Hai, said, "In seeing matter, you are at the same time seeing mind. Without the arising of the object, the subject does not arise." When our mind is conscious of something, we *are* that thing. When we contemplate a snow-covered mountain, we are that mountain. When we watch a noisy film, we are that noisy film.

Our mind is like a television set with thousands of channels, and the channel we switch on is the channel we are at that moment. When we turn on anger, we are anger. When we turn on peace and joy, we are peace and joy. We have the ability to select the channel. *We are what we choose to be.* W e can select any channel of the mind. Buddha is a channel, Mara is a channel, remembering is a channel, forgetting is a channel, calm is a channel, agitation is a channel. Changing from one state of being to another is as simple as the change from a channel showing a film to a channel playing music.

There are people who cannot tolerate peace and quiet, who are afraid of facing themselves, so they turn on the television in order to be preoccupied with it for a whole evening. In contemporary culture, people rarely like to be with themselves, and they frequently seek forgetfulness—downtown at the theater or other places of amusement. People rarely like to look deeply and compassionately at themselves. Young people in America watch television more than five hours per day, and they also have all sorts of electronic games to occupy them. Where will a culture in which people do not have the chance to face themselves or form real relationships with others lead us?

There are many interesting, instructive programs on television, and we can use the TV guide to select programs which encourage mindfulness. We should decide to watch only the programs we have selected and avoid becoming a victim of the television.

48. DRIVING THE CAR

Before starting the car,
I know where I am going.
The car and I are one.
If the car goes fast, I go fast.

In *Being Peace,* I explained these four lines. If we are mindful when we start our car, we will know how to use it properly. When we are driving, we tend to think of arriving, and we sacrifice the journey for the sake of the arrival. But life is to be found in the present moment, not in the future. In fact, we may suffer more after we arrive at our destination. If we have to talk of a destination, what about our final destination, the graveyard? We do not want to go in the direction of death; we want to go to in the direction of life. But where is life? Life can be found only in the present moment. Therefore, each mile we drive, each step we take, has to bring us into the present moment. This is the practice of mindfulness.

When we see a red light or a stop sign, we can smile at it and thank it, because it is a bodhisattva helping us return to the present moment. The red light is a bell of mindfulness. We may have thought of it as an enemy, preventing us from achieving our goal. But now we know the red light is our friend, helping us resist rushing and calling us to return to the present moment where we can meet with life, joy, and peace. Even if you are not the driver, you can help everyone in the car if you breathe and smile.

A number of years ago, I went to Canada to lead a retreat, and a friend took me across the city of Montréal. I noticed that every time a car stopped in front of me, I saw the sentence, *"Je me souviens"* ("I remember"), on the license plate. I did not know what they wanted to remember, perhaps their French-speaking origin, but it gave me an idea. I told my friend, "I have a present for all of you here. Every time you see a car stop in front of you with the line '*Je me souviens*,' you can see it as a bell of mindfulness helping you remember to breathe and smile. And you will have plenty of opportunities to breathe and smile while driving in Montréal."

My friend was delighted! He liked it so much that he shared the practice with more than 200 people in the retreat. Later, when he came to visit me in France, he told me that Paris was not a good place to practice driving, as there were no signs, "*Je me souviens*." I told him that he could practice with red lights and stop signs. After he left Plum Village and went back to Montréal, he wrote me a beautiful letter: "Thây, practicing in Paris was very easy. Not only did I practice with red lights and stop signs, but every time a car stopped in front of me, I saw the eyes of the Buddha blinking at me. I had to smile at those blinking eyes."

The next time you are caught in traffic, don't fight. It is useless to fight. If you sit back and smile to yourself, you will enjoy the present moment and make everyone in the car happy. The Buddha is there, because the Buddha can always be found in the present moment. Practicing meditation is to return to the present moment in order to encounter the flower, the blue sky, the child, the brilliant red light.

49. TURNING ON THE LIGHT

Forgetfulness is the darkness;
mindfulness is the light.
I bring awareness
to shine upon all life.

When you touch a light switch, you can stop for a few seconds to recite this gatha before you turn on the light. Not only will there be light in the room, but there will also be light within you. Dwelling in the present moment is a miracle. Every illusion and random thought will disappear, just as darkness disappears when the light comes on. When we are mindful, we get in touch with the refreshing, peaceful, healing elements within ourselves and around us. Peace and joy are available anytime.

Conscious breathing helps us return to the present moment. I practice breathing every day. In my small meditation room, I have calligraphed the sentence, "Breathe, you are alive!" When mindfulness shines its light upon our activity, we recover ourselves and encounter life in the present moment. The present moment is a wonderful moment.

Parallax Press publishes books on Buddhism and related subjects to make them accessible and alive for contemporary readers. We carry all books and tapes by Thich Nhat Hanh, as well as *Happy Veggies*, by Mayumi Oda. For a copy of our free catalog, please write to:

Parallax Press
P. O. Box 7355
Berkeley, California 94707

About the Author

Thich Nhat Hanh, Vietnamese Zen master, poet, and peace activist, has been a monk for nearly 50 years. In Vietnam, he founded the School of Youth for Social Service ("the little peace corps"), an instrument for re-building villages that were destroyed by bombs and for resettling tens of thousands of people fleeing the war zones. He also founded Van Hanh Buddhist University, La Boi Press, and the Tiep Hien Order of Interbeing. In 1966, he came to the U.S. and Europe at the invitation of the Fellowship of Reconciliation to "represent the wishes of the Vietnamese people of all faiths who had no means to speak for themselves" (*New Yorker*, June 25, 1966). He was nominated by Martin Luther King, Jr. for the Nobel Peace Prize in 1967. Unable to return to Viet-nam after his overseas tour, he received asylum in France, where he served as chairman of the Vietnamese Buddhist Peace Delegation to the Paris Peace Talks. He lives in Plum Village, a small community in France, where he continues teaching, writing, gardening, and helping refugees worldwide.

About the Artist

Mayumi Oda, born in Japan, is an internationally recog-nized artist. Her bold contemporary imagery has been identified with the work of Matisse. She has had many one-woman exhibits in Japan and the U.S., and her work is in the permanent collections of the Museum of Modern Art in New York, the Museum of Fine Arts in Boston, and the Library of Congress. She is the author of *Goddesses* and *Happy Veggies*, and she has contributed the covers to many books, including *The Tassajara Bread Book*, *Turning the Wheel*, and *Not Mixing Up Buddhism*. Ms. Oda lives and works near the Green Gulch Zen Center, just north of San Francisco.